101 Words to
Save the World

Published by Mary Strickland
© Mary Strickland
All rights reserved. No part of this publication may be reproduced
or transmitted by any means including electronic, mechanical,
photocopying or otherwise, without prior permission of the author.

ISBN: 978-0-9576249-3-1

Design: www.istudio21.co.uk
The information in this book is based on information from *The
Wildlife Trust, Compassion in World Farming, Respect for
Animals, The Day* newspaper for schools and other news stories.

For Walter, who loved the natural world

101 Words to Save the World

The idea for this book originated in an experimental
entry for a short story competition where the limit
was 100 words. I didn't think it was possible to write
anything meaningful with such limitations, but I learned
that when you have so few words you have to get to the
point quickly and it helps if the subject is something you
feel strongly about.

Soon afterwards I wrote another one and the idea was
born for a series of soundbites, any one of which could
help to change the world for the better if the implicit
messages got through.

101 words… addresses the impact of humans on other
living creatures and on the environment in an accessible
way that can be read from cover to cover or simply
dipped in to. It is aimed not only at those who care about
other living creatures, but also to those who don't care—
in the hope that they may change.

The overall message is twofold—that we have to save
the natural world by changing the way we live and that
we need to empathise more with other living creatures.
It will take incentive, purpose and passion at grass roots
level, but everyone can make a difference.

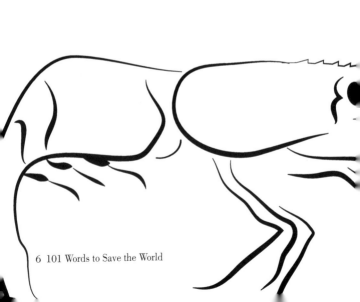

Legacy to die for

We live in a throwaway society. For decades plastic shopping bags were used for an average of just 12 minutes before being discarded and even most new clothes have long been cheap and tacky because the fashion world likes a fast turnover. Discarded plastic kills at least a million seabirds every year—together with 100,000 or so sea mammals—and we are told that there will be more plastic than fish in the oceans by 2050. If the world survives in any form our legacy is likely to be layers of plastic choking the life out of anything that moves.

Rat Trap

The tortures of poison are approved in controlling us and no one cares when we languish in 'humane' traps for days on end. Yet, if humans were any other breed, they would be the ones to be controlled as pests, for there is no species more destructive and prolific. I would never have chosen to be born a rat, but I would far less be human.

Acid stomach

Vultures can eat even creatures with anthrax and rabies, thanks to their super strong stomach acid which rivals hydrochloric acid. Without them, dangerous diseases would spread to man and beast alike, as happened in India when the vulture population dipped 99 per cent over a ten year period, resulting in an increase of 150,000 human deaths from rabies. These amazing birds protect our eco system, yet they are frequently considered unattractive and despised as scavengers. Perhaps it would have been better if we had all died off long ago and left the vultures to clear up after us.

Another line crossed

In a mind-bending parody of itself, the real fur industry has in recent years been passing off real fur as fake fur. The television programme *Fake Britain* found fur from five animals—Racoon, fox, weasel, mink and rabbit—on cheap High Street clothing where the labels either omitted any mention of fur or actually passed off the real fur as fake. Quite apart from the moral quagmire this exposes, the commercial effect is to artificially inflate the price of real fur, to the detriment of millions of animal victims who are variously caged, maimed, gassed, strangled, trapped and electrocuted.

As you sow...

External shocks such as superbugs, killer robots and
nuclear war are among criteria which could catapult
us permanently back to the Stone Age, according to
research at the University of Cambridge. Climate
change, environmental abuse and our globalised
economic system are also factors and our potential
demise is compared to the Roman Empire—one of the
greatest civilisations ever—which took only 86 years
to collapse. Looking on the bright side, a return to the
Stone Age might work wonders for the endemic bad
manners and consumerism of the 21st century.

The bandwaggon

African governments are cheerfully selling off land to
foreigners who want it for growing crops and neither
party has any regard for the tribes, local residents or
wildlife already in occupation. In their haste to sign, the
Ethiopian government didn't even notice that one project
ran right through a wildlife reserve created to protect an
endangered species of antelope. Luckily the boundaries
were re-drawn, but not every creature affected is so
lucky. In Africa as a whole, 80 million hectares of
land were sold for crops in a single year, 2008-2009.
'Destroyed in haste, repented at leisure' may become the
epitaph of a generation.

A view to a kill

In April 2017 a documentary about a 14 year old boy in America described how he shot both of his puritanical, middle class parents three times each in the head as they slept. Inexplicably, both survived. The family were hunters—the boy had already shot deer and his mother had shot her first deer when she was 12. After being diagnosed with a major depressive disorder he said it was a relief to know that he wasn't 'crazy, or an animal, or anything like that'. Point number 1: People who show violence to animals usually don't stop there. Point number 2: Why would anyone use 'animal' as a term of abuse?

Beasts of burden

Lucy Fensom worked as a flight attendant with *British Airways* for four years with the goal of raising enough money to open a sanctuary for working and abandoned donkeys in the Israel. In 1999 she took in a foal whose mother had been killed on a busy road and so began many years of overcoming the insurmountable. Next was three legged Cachou and then Jordy who had been marched through the streets of Jericho during an anti-Israel protest and had his ears and tail chopped off. For some people charity starts at home, but at a distance the suffering is often even greater.

Safe Haven for Donkeys in the Holy Land (SHADH)

Beginning over

In 2015 Lucy left SHADH (opposite) and started
Lucy's Sanctuary for Holy Land Donkeys on an area of
Palestinian ground in Israel. However, the new premises
were in a rough area and she was forced to move again.
After many knocks along the way, a charity in England
called Lucy's UK Donkey Foundation was set up in 2017
and they pay the rent as well as sending whatever equine
supplies they can afford. It's good to know that there are
still people willing to sacrifice an easy life for the cause
they believe in.

Trench warfare

Millionaire American explorer Victor Vescovo broke the record for the deepest ever solo dive when he descended 10,927 metres to the bottom of the *Mariana Trench* in the Pacific Ocean and found…a plastic bag and some sweet wrappers. That wasn't all, of course, but it underlines how not even the world's most remote sanctuary is safe from human intrusion. A devastating 13 million metric tons of plastic ends up in the oceans each year and it is up to individuals to re-think our throwaway culture.

Death by plastic

Everybody knows that plastic pollution kills sea life, but it also kills around 1 million people every year—predominantly in poor countries which don't have the infrastructure to dispose of it. As a result it ends up in the environment and becomes a breeding ground for disease-spreading mosquitoes or alternatively it blocks drains and causes flooding and cholera. Sometimes the plastic is burned and gives off toxic fumes which cause air pollution and contribute to climate change. Only the companies who export plastic to those countries can provide the solution, but it will mean putting the planet above their profits.

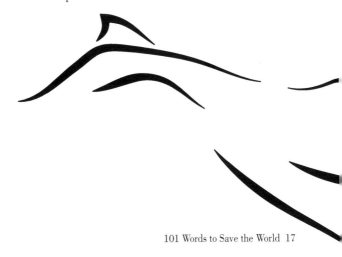

Asia has a problem with dogs

In Asia 30 million dogs a year are killed for human consumption in the most brutal ways. Most are family pets or village dogs cared for collectively by the community and anyone who speaks out can expect reprisal attacks from the machete wielding thugs who carry out the thefts. The dogs are then transported thousands of miles for slaughter, with many dying of heat stroke or exhaustion en route, before finally the survivors watch terrified as other dogs are drowned, bludgeoned to death or set on fire in front of them. Burning is a convenient way to get rid of fur.

Brave New World

Incredibly, 1,412 live tigers were exported from the European Union between 1999-2016 for purposes ranging from tourism to circuses or slaughter for traditional medicine. The UK, France, Belgium and the Netherlands are among the countries involved in this business—worth £45 million annually—and despite calls by the charity *Four Paws* to ban the trade, they have so far failed to act. Unfortunately the western world frequently ignores atrocities in countries with whom it suits them to do business, which is a depressing indictment. The mantra may change, but human nature doesn't.

Blinded by greed

In the *Leuser* rainforest in Sumatra, Indonesia, palm oil farmers are shooting orangutans displaced by the new crops. One injured animal captured by a charity had been shot 62 times while another had been completely blinded and would have to remain in captivity for the rest of its life. Farmers aim for the face because a blind orangutan will starve to death and for reasons best known to themselves they also aim for the groin. Leuser is one of the most biodiverse places on earth but has lost 110,000 hectares of forest in the last 20 years, with animals trapped even as the forest is obliterated around them.

The gentler sex

David Attenborough has warned of irreversible damage
to the natural world and the collapse of our societies.
There are those who wouldn't care about the former,
but hopefully even they would be concerned by the
latter, in case, God forbid, they might be personally
affected. Like the woman in Sumatra, who in reference
to the destruction of the *Leuser* forest for palm oil crops
said, 'What's more important, humans or orangutans?
If it matters that much, take them to forests in other
countries.' On the other hand, a native charity worker
was close to tears as he spoke of the human expression
in the eyes of the displaced animals.

New Intelligence

It is intriguing to see collaborations of mutual love and respect between working animals and humans, but the concept has been taken to unexpected and cynical lengths in some military circles. In April 1919 a group of Norwegian fishermen discovered a friendly beluga whale wearing a harness with *Equipment of St Petersburg* written on it. Things have come on a bit since Russian recruitment of dolphins in the 1980s for… what? Potential uses included carrying poison darts, laying underwater mines, locating enemy fighters or even destroying submarines—Kamikaze style. Not much love lost there.

Ingenious animal recruitment

The Russians are not alone in their harnessing of marine intelligence, as the US trains both dolphins and sea lions. Meanwhile, in 2011 Saudi Police arrested a vulture on suspicion that it was working for Israel's infamous secret police and the same agency was also blamed for a spate of shark attacks near the Red Sea resort of Sharm el-Sheikh in 2010—the cause was said to be GPS controlled predators planted to harm the Egyptian tourist industry. On a more positive note, cormorants help fishermen catch…fish in Japan, while in Thailand trained monkeys climb hundreds of feet to pick coconuts.

More ingenious animal recruitment

In 2007 a team of 14 'Spy Squirrels' was famously arrested by the Iranian army near a nuclear enrichment plant, 'before they could take any action'. Planted by..? Meanwhile the CIA came up with *Operation Accoustic Kitty* in which listening devices were implanted into a cat, although the project came to a premature end on Day 1 when the unfortunate feline was run over by a car outside the Soviet Embassy in Washington.

Another failed American project was the WW2 use of bats who were ruthlessly strapped to incendiary devices and dropped over Japan, where it was hoped that they would burst into flames while roosting inside wooden buildings.

The Natural Order

Our relationship with other living creatures is multi-layered. We experiment on them, hunt them for sport, use them for transport or labour and kill them for fur or meat in programmes of gruesome mass murder. Any impartial observer could hardly deny that humans are the most self-interested, thankless and violent of animals, yet happily there are also a few formidable collaborations for good: dogs working for the Police, Prison officers, Customs or the Army, Guide dogs, Hearing dogs…and without Carrier Pigeons we might not have won two world wars. All the same, it is hard to celebrate when the scales probably come down at around 80% exploitation.

Natural greatness

Even the legend himself—David Attenborough—admits that we are not going to be in time to save all of the animal kingdom and nor are we going to be able to do enough. At one of the public events launching his television series *Our Planet* he said, 'We won't be able to mend everything, but we can make it a darn sight better than it would be if we didn't do anything at all…We owe it to our ancestors who brought us this far and to the natural world, to give back as much as possible of what we have stolen.'

Tomorrow's World

Climate change has caused the Greenland ice sheet to lose four trillion tonnes of ice—five times as fast as was the case 25 years ago. These losses are driving up sea levels around the world and in the US, low-lying Louisiana is losing land at the rate of a football field every 45 minutes. Technology is catching up with the problem but not fast enough: for instance, wind energy is now as cheap as fossil fuels and carbon dioxide can be extracted from the air by large machines, turned to stone and buried underground. It may sound futuristic, but these and other fledgling technologies are a vital part of preserving what is left of the natural world.

The end of the world as we know it

Climate change in brief is the effect when gases like methane and carbon dioxide are released into the atmosphere. These work like a greenhouse, trapping the Earth's heat and raising its average temperature. The result of this attack on the planet's equilibrium is scorching temperatures, freak snowstorms, wildfires, earthquakes and rising seas. According to NASA the global temperature has risen by 1 degree C since the 1950s and don't be deceived by that low figure—Earth was only 4 degrees cooler in the Ice Age. The two most effective things you can do to counter it are—in order of importance—stop eating meat and buy an electric car.

Where cow meats climate change

So what is the connection between eating meat and contributing to the destruction of the natural world? The problems are intensive meat farming and the link with palm oil and soya crops. In short: thousands of forests and animal grazing land are destroyed to plant these crops and the loss of the trees causes an increase in levels of carbon dioxide—the second most abundant contributor to global warming. In a system clearly designed by a lunatic, about 90% of the soya crops are then used to feed unhappy animal victims of intensive farming—many of whom have been displaced by those same crops. Meanwhile, palm oil is used in countless supermarket products from onion granules to chocolate. Check the labels before you buy.

The race that threw it all away

American entomologist William Wheeler has a
depressing view of the future of our civilization. He
likens the eventual state of human society to that
currently enjoyed by termites and explains the analogy
as follows: 'They have very low intelligence combined
with an intense and pugnacious solidarity of the whole.'
Historically individualism is the reason that humans
have thrived and collectivism has been detrimental to
progress, so does this mean that 21st century political
correctness and the vigilance of a controlling social
media is turning us all into blithering idiots?

Castles in the sky

It seems that what termites lack in character they make up for in other ways. Their bulbous, eyeless heads and translucent bodies are not endearing, yet they are hugely industrious and the 30 foot mounds which they spend their lives building include intricate designs of tunnels, archways and even spiral staircases. However, the function of these masterpieces is only to enable the termites to breathe from the place they really call home—which is somewhere in the ground beneath. Furthermore, they don't sleep, can convert dead plant matter into energy and their ethos of the collective before the individual has its merits. Each to his own.

Children of a lesser God

Indian elephant, Mohan, spent 50 years performing at weddings and was 150 stone underweight when finally rescued in September 2016. He was only a few months from death. His release by *Wildlife SOS* came after more than two years of evasion by his cruel owner and was compounded by countless court delays and even the threats of a 300 strong mob. Abscesses and countless scars are among the legacies of his imprisonment, spiked leg chains one of his enduring memories. Thus has commerce eclipsed any protection once afforded by religious and cultural significance.

There are more than 3,500 working elephants in India and tourists should boycott all elephant rides and performances.

The highest and lowest forms of life

An elephant who suffered alongside Mohan was Raja,
and they may have been illegally poached together.
When Raja was rescued in July 2014 both elephants
were owned by members of the same family, but from
capture he had changed hands at least 27 times during
his 50+ years of captivity, enduring the initiation 'crush'
each time. Badly starved, he had been reduced to
eating cardboard and plastic. His last, depraved owner
screamed at him to attack the 36-strong rescue team but
instead, daring to hope for the first time, the elephant
wept tears of joy as he shuffled painfully to their lorry,
his spiked chains biting at every step.

Raja's dangerous rescue by the *Wildlife SOS* team was
of necessity supported by 20 forestry officials and six
policemen.

Cecil

My eyes were melting pots of fire, my roar immense and my magnificent, black mane flowed wild and free.
I knew of humans, but feared no-one. And then one day a criminal came in the dark and tricked me with meat dragged from a truck. I followed the scent and from nowhere white treachery rent my body apart. Cursed by strength I ran, and the sun came and went twice until finally another roar broke the silence and my spirit soared.

Other people's lives

Dammit, I've got money and an ego to go with it. Shame the brute didn't cop it with a bow and arrow, but what the hell. As soon as I saw him I knew he was the one for me and it's easy to get what you want by the back door in Africa. Straight off, I knew that magnificent head and black mane would look much better on my hearth than on his mangy body. Whatever floats your boat—know what I mean?

In memory of Cecil, the Zimbabwean lion illegally hunted in 2015 by American dentist Walter Palmer. He was mortally wounded with a bow and arrow, then shot, beheaded and skinned two days later.

Bravado v the brave

The most important scientific evidence regarding badgers and tuberculosis comes from the *Randomised Badger Culling Trial*, also known as the *Krebs Trial*, which ran from 1998 to 2005. It was funded by the Government and compared the effects of culling across ten sites in England. It stated: 'On the basis of our careful review of all currently available evidence, we conclude that badger culling is unlikely to contribute positively or cost effectively to the control of Cattle TB in Britain.' So having commissioned the report and got the answer they didn't want, the government ignored it anyway.

Braveheart

We are blessed with great strength and stamina, God-given, but exploited by evil men with twisted minds. We never win, because when we beat the terriers, they send new ones down into our sets. Inflated with cruelty, these humans demean all of their kind. Yet we have enemies even beyond these murderers and their dogs—those who believe that we spread TB among cattle, although science refutes it. Bullets fired in the dark do not kill us painlessly, nor spare our unborn young. We are the walking wounded in a war against ignorance, where reason and beauty count for nothing.

Badgers have been defenceless victims of a government waging a PR war in an attempt to appease angry farmers.

Crime and punishment

Poaching is worth around £650 million a year and is the fourth most lucrative criminal activity internationally. Elephants are brutally slaughtered for their ivory which is worth $1,000 for a half kilo and rhino horn is more valuable than gold or platinum. Tigers are killed for their pelts and great apes and exotic birds are sold as pets— usually to people with no idea how to care for them. It is all driven by humanity's basest impulses for status symbols and trophies. Make a stand and burn your ivory heirlooms on behalf of the civilised world.

Compound evil

There is no defence against the poaching of wild and often endangered animals in Africa, but some apologists claim that natives are driven to it in desperation as progress deprives them of an income. Forget that. The new generation of poachers uses AK-47 machine guns, rocket launchers and helicopters which are not only turned on the animals but also on the rangers who protect them. In the ten years up to 2016, more than 1,000 rangers were killed in 35 different countries and the resultant profits shared between militia groups, crime syndicates and terrorist organisations. The degradation of man is a far cry from the beauty of the natural world.

Big brother

The Thai mahout grinned ingratiatingly at the camera from an elephant logging park in Thailand. 'We love the elephants, they are our livelihood,' he insisted—a precursor to giving himself a big pat on the back for organising a feast day to celebrate elephants. 'Sometimes we have to beat them when the work is heavy,' he mused, almost as if it were a good thing. Rods, chains and metal hooks are the instruments of choice and so brutal is the week long Pajan initiation that half of the baby elephants subjected to it are literally beaten to death in the process.

Cursed race

Sanjay Gandhi National Park in India is 40 square miles of green space in Mumbai, an over-populated city of nearly 21 million people who in the last 50 years have encroached upon 85 per cent of the wild habitat surrounding them. There are still 35 magnificent leopards who live in and around the park in greatly reduced circumstances and this was the fate of one of them—maybe more. Trapped, doused with kerosene and filmed as it writhed and died in a ball of fire. I can think of no more fitting atrocity for which a human soul would be eternally damned.

Debenham Vicarage

Hens came from next door and laid eggs in the hollow tree on the driveway, while a duck nested each year under my mother's gooseberry bushes, next to the washing line. There were pinks in the flower beds and cow parsley burgeoned along the long drive. Lizards settled under rough stones bordering the kitchen lawn and wild bees made a corner of the roof their hive of industry in nature's rich tapestry. The wild pond at the back was full of frog spawn, the acacia tree on the front lawn embraced the honeysuckle and the giant cedar guarded my father's study. Now everything and everyone is dead, except for me.

El Niño

Nestled in a bush where my mother had hidden us, we escaped the worst of the heat and turned our heads away from the flies. Blinded by disease I saw nothing, but every day a strange food was left, melting in the summer sun. Starving and alone, we ate what we could, close to death. Then one day a woman took us away and other cats watched as our eyes were bathed and a woman said in a soft voice, 'Es un niño'.

A group of kittens in the summer of 2010, fed on Roquefort cheese by the porter of a block of flats in Málaga until they were rescued and taken to the refuge PAD at Mijas Costa in Spain. Translation: 'It's a boy.'

Enigmas of the sea

Our majesty disguises a fragility which is at odds with our size and power. Sensitive and complex, we traverse the oceans and enrich our world.

We have long endured terrible deaths inflicted by man, but now we have another enemy—armies in the sea bed and echoes which never cease. Disorientated we try to escape, but the noise fogs our brains.

Frantic, we swim for days—never stopping, never feeding—until we are washed up on a foreign shore to die. Surrounded by curious humans.

Research shows that constant noise produced by wind farms and gas exploration is causing some whales to panic.

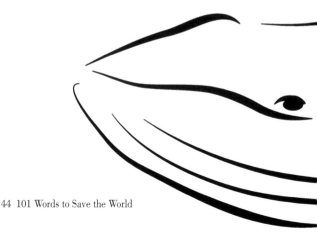

Wind swept

A huge volume of underwater sounds of varying intensity and duration are generated from offshore wind turbines during construction, operation and decommissioning. During construction there is seismic exploration using airguns, excavation with explosives, dredging, ship operations and disturbance of the sea bed to build foundations. As a turbine operates, vibrations are transmitted down the main shaft and to the seafloor, increasing slightly with wind speed. I'm not saying there shouldn't be wind turbines because they are an important breakthrough in renewable energy, but at what cost to the marine life they invade?

Food for thought

Putting aside for a moment whatever genetic similarities exist between pigs and humans, how many of us have ever considered the physical characteristics we have in common? For instance, we both have hairless skin, protruding noses, heavy eyelashes and—in the western world—predominantly light coloured eyes. For some years now, pig skin tissues and heart valves have been used in medicine because of their compatibility with the human body. Instead of taking the name of the pig in vain, it would be much more appropriate to revere the animal as our much maligned and misunderstood benefactor.

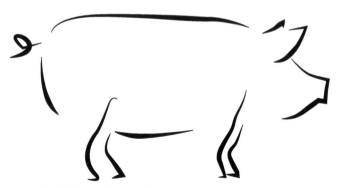

Espie

There is nothing more calculated to weigh on the conscience of animalistas than the animals they fail, and my first failure was a female ginger kitten-cat called Espie. She lived in a colony of 15 or so cats in *Cerrado de Calderón*, Málaga, where I was living, and although one or two local residents fed them, she was very thin. I wanted to take her but allowed myself to be dissuaded until a few months down the line, by which time it was too late. She was already pregnant and with a colon tumour, which explained her diminishing weight. She died under anaesthetic.

Excess baggage

The Day is an electronic newspaper for schools and at the end of the four or five daily articles they always have what is called a short epic, which is usually a humorous one-liner telling a true story or fact. However, today, under the humorous headline *Excess Baggage* is the following: 'A strange discovery this weekend inside four checked-in suitcases at Manila's Ninoy Aquino airport — 1,529 live turtles. All are well.' It might be funny if it wasn't so sad.

March 2019

Fact and fiction

Since time began there has existed a biblical edict that man is the most important animal and therefore has dominion over the food, territory and even existence of other creatures. Some apologists attempt to explain away this imbalance of power with the jaded observation that it has always been like that, or with the old chestnut about animals not experiencing emotion on the same scale as us, so perhaps after all, they don't really mind the emotional and physical pain we inflict on them. Increasingly these myths are shot to pieces before our eyes, so where does that leave us?

Enlightenment

On Christmas Eve 2017 I fulfilled a long held intention
of picking up plastic wrappers, broken glass and God
knows what else, which over time had become embedded
in the hedges and turf of our village recreation ground.
I filled several bin bags with all that I found and since
then have maintained my vigil. I have crawled on my
stomach through thorny hedges, ripped my clothes
and ripped my hands, but I am sustained by the
fantasy of waving a magic wand and incarcerating the
morons responsible in a padded cell for days at a time,
interrupting their solace only to ask at intervals if they
have any idea why they are there.

Forty dumb animals

One poster said,' It takes up to 40 dumb animals to make a fur coat, but only one to wear it.' And another said simply: 'Rich bitch, poor bitch.' Purveyors of real fur in fashion had some semblance of excuse in the past because pre-1980s there wasn't the same awareness, but amazingly there are still some designers, models and members of the public buying into this anachronistic hell on earth for its animal victims. Even now, it seems, there is in some quarters a twisted sort of glamour in wearing fur—if you've got the stomach for it.

Going bust

The price of mink and fox skins fell by around 22% in 2018 and with it the wealth of *Saga Furs*, who went from a profit of nearly 27 million euros in 2013 to a loss of 1.7 million six years later…. However, the number of pelts they sold was still more than 9.3 million, so all those animals suffered and died just for the company to make a significant loss—but thank God it did. What used to be a fur empire is now the ragged remains of a mercenary army, but what remains will fight to the death. I hope I live to see it.

Going down

Confirming the financial woes of the fur trade, the world's largest fur auction house ended its February 2019 auction with an average price of £19 for each pelt. *Kopenhagen Furs* is owned by Danish fur breeders and given that each skin has to sell for £35 for a fur breeder to even break even, the slashed prices thankfully indicate a serious economic outlook for the industry.

The ginger one

You were a ginger blob when I rescued you from *Parque Sanitario* in Málaga, and what adventures we've had. You immediately got the deadly kitten virus and it took Rafa five days to bring you back to life. Then my bad Spanish got me into hot water and you were shipped off to an animal refuge by mistake. 'Go with the flow' I thought. But six weeks later you were still there and I reclaimed you. 'Guapíssssimo,' said the lady who handed you over, for a fee. Yes, handsome to a fault. And you're still here. An oasis of calm in a chaotic world.

Grass roots

People for the Ethical Treatment of Animals—otherwise
known as PETA—is a UK based charity with over 1,700
cruelty free companies on its database, of which one
is the Body Shop, founded by Anita Roddick in 1976.
Using naturally scented products it was an instant hit
and when she sold the business in 2006 it was reported
that she made £130 million from the sale. She said at the
time that the best thing about having money was being
able to give it away, but tragically died only a year later.
Even so, her example and legacy live on.

My friend, the whale

Whaling is a barbaric process by any standards, and all the worse in the light of the advanced culture and communication enjoyed by whales. They have different dialects and communities and pass information from generation to generation through whale song. One research project witnessed Humpback whales on different sides of Australia singing complex, different songs, but when one group heard the other via echolocation, they instantly changed their own song to match the other one exactly. Alarmingly, Blue Whale research indicates that noise pollution has caused a reduction in hearing capacity from 1000 miles in 1940 to 100 miles today—undoing 25 million years of evolution.

Whale of a massacre

In the four months November 2017-March 2018, Japan killed 333 Minke whales in the Antarctic, of which 122 were pregnant females and a further 114 were not yet adults. They then announced in December 2018 that they were withdrawing from the *International Whaling Commission* which had banned commercial whaling in 1986, although the agreement had left an unfortunate scientific research clause which the Japanese exploited with unashamed transparency. Using this loophole they killed 18,000 Sperm, Sei, Bryde and Minke whales over the 33 years of the agreement, but at least in future they will only be able to massacre their own waters.

Feathered apes

The corvid family—of which crows, rooks, jackdaws, jays and magpies are some of the best known—are very intelligent and their advanced cognitive abilities enable them to synchronise and adapt in order to overcome problems. Their skills even include 'delayed gratification', which is a rare quality in the animal world and enables those who possess it to deny themselves an immediate reward in anticipation of long term benefit. For example, they bury food in the full knowledge that it will be there when there is less food to be had—and hopefully with the desirable addition of maggots.

Bats...

Repair broken DNA and never get cancer
Have been using sonar for 50 million years as compared
to our 100 years
Live in communities (sometimes up to c.15 million)
On a daily basis use team work, huddle together for
warmth, share food and groom each other
Can live to be up to 40 years old
Have much to teach us.

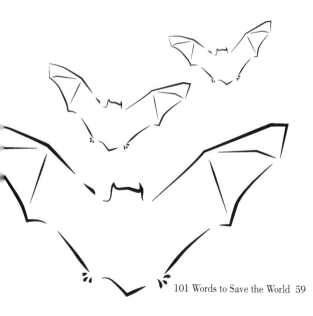

Heroes and villains

Mark Glover is the director of anti-fur campaigning charity *Respect for Animals* and for years has been putting his money where his mouth is in attacking the trade which traps, strangles, gases, electrocutes and cages animals in the name of fashion. In 1992 he was made bankrupt when a court case went against him after he described a mink farm as a 'hell hole', only to be curiously contradicted by an RSPCA inspector. Nevertheless, *Respect's* 'Case against fur factory farming' says it all in tragic pictures where even disfigurement cannot disguise great beauty and nobility.

The good, the bad and the ugly

In 1994 supermodel Naomi Campbell starred in a poster for *People for the Ethical Treatment of Animals* (PETA) when she posed naked with four other models for a poster reading, 'We'd rather go naked than wear fur.' It's now old news that Ms Campbell modelled a sable coat three years later, followed it up with further transgressions and later said that her part in the campaign was 'a mistake'. She was sacked by the charity but appears unmoved by criticism, including that of celebrity Pamela Anderson who in 2017 sent a private message reminding her that the many of the animals she wore had been anally electrocuted or skinned alive.

Going, going, gone...

There were five kittens mewling joyfully but hungrily outside my Spanish flat. It was May and someone had abandoned them. Late that evening I caught all but one and I hadn't the heart to leave him alone, so put them all back until the following day when I could try again. Terrible mistake—the cat catchers came early next morning. I rang them. 'Fifteen days quarantine, then you can have them,' said an indifferent voice. I rang again. 'They all died,' said another indifferent voice. *Parque Sanitario* in Ciudad Jardin, Malaga, wasn't fit to be a slaughterhouse, far less a municipal refuge.

May 2004

The great deception

Kitana, the black rhino, carried her baby for sixteen months and was overjoyed after giving birth, but her joy turned to despair after only six weeks when the female calf died of a heart defect. Heartbroken she searched for her, uttering little squeaks. Finally she sank into a deep and lasting depression. In a world where Emperor penguins become frantic if they lose their chick in the melee of the breeding ground, where elephants weep tears and pigs sing lullabies to their children, how could we ever doubt that their emotions and sensitivities are every bit as deep and complex as our own?

Growing old

I was young and knew nothing of life until that day when the man put a rope around my neck and dragged me away. I whimpered and he swore, then the world I knew disappeared in a cloud of dust as I cowered in a metal trailer. He left me among trees and grass and my spirits lifted in the absence of his dark soul. Eagerly I explored, too innocent to know that beauty can disguise great evil, but when the cold, steel jaws sprang shut, I grew old.

For Bella, 2005-2016. Born in Cabra, near Córdoba, Spain

Helping bees to save the world

Bees love purple flowers best of all as they see
them more clearly, but here is a guide to some other
favourites. In a few cases their flowering periods overlap
the seasons, but a handful from any category could make
a world of difference to our beleaguered bees.

Spring: bluebell, cherry, crab apple, daffodil, forget-
me-not, hawthorn, hyacinth, rhododendron, rosemary,
snowdrop.

Early summer: allium, comfrey, fennel, foxglove, hardy
geranium, honeysuckle, iris, snap dragon, teasel, thyme,
verbascum.

Late summer: angelica, aster, buddleia, cornflower,
dahlia, fuchsia, globe thistle, heather, ivy, lavender,
penstemon, verbena bonariensis.

Heroes

The late vet, Buster Lloyd Jones (1914-80) had an instinct for diagnosis and after becoming too ill to practice, described losing this gift as 'like a light being switched off'. He took his herbal remedies and instruments everywhere and on hearing a cow lowing in pain while on holiday in Corsica, he sought her out. The farmer was delighted when he offered his services free of charge and the cow was particularly affectionate and grateful. Over the following two weeks they became firm friends, so how great was his distress when he learned that she was to be slaughtered the day after he left.

The story of Buster L-J was immortalised in his books, 'The Animals Came in One by One' and 'Come into my World'.

High interest

There was a place full of meat that I longed to enter, but I was afraid because the humans inside were fierce and greedy. Days passed and I grew weaker, but one day hunger overcame my fear and I darted in, snatched a meal and ran. For days I stayed away, but hunger tempted me back. Tense but resolute I inched over the threshold and from nowhere came an explosion of noise and pain as the man lunged forward, metal flashing. I paid my debt with interest.

A World Animal Protection Association report featured a butcher who attacked a hungry dog with a meat cleaver.

Home from home

A man remarked in passing that three years previously
he had filled in a wetland area in his garden because
'it wasn't doing much'. So he was surprised when the
following year a clutch of frog spawn appeared in the
middle of the newly grassed area which had previously
been the precious, marshy swamp beloved of a pair
of frogs. My first response was to be deeply moved by
the frogs' determination that their habitual nesting site
should prevail and my second was disappointment and
incomprehension at his complete lack of any remorse for
what he had done.

Homeless

Since 1970 humans have destroyed 60% of the world's wildlife and many scientists say that we are already in the midst of earth's sixth mass extinction. There is a feeling of hopelessness that it is already too late and that there will never be enough people sufficiently interested to make a difference, but everyone owes it to the planet to do what they can—personally and financially. David Attenborough's *Our Planet* features an orangutan playing in a Borneo jungle, followed by time-lapse footage of the same forest being destroyed for palm oil plantations. No-one needs more reason than that to come out of the shadows.

How far have we come?

The report of the Rome and Neapolitan *Societies for the Protection of Animals* for the first half of the year 1908 revealed that 974 prosecutions had been undertaken in Rome and 1,992 in Naples. Also that 2,627 instruments of torture had been recovered by the society's agents in Rome and 8588 in the Southern capital. The number of vehicles whose loads had been lightened or adjusted by them was 9,529 and 30,946 in Naples. Finally, 516 incurably diseased dogs and cats were placed in the lethal chambers of Rome and 403 in those of Naples.

From the Rome correspondent of the Observer newspaper.

I wish...

...that elephants ruled the world and that all violent and manipulative humans would cease to be. That all the environmental damage man has done could be undone and that all our ugly constructions would crumble to dust. That fundamentalism didn't exist and that freedom was taken for granted. That the consumption, killing and imprisonment of other living creatures by humans was an anathema to all and that the human population was more than halved. And that technological advances had ended in the 1930s and assisted dying was legal. Only then could I say, what a truly, truly wonderful world.

Ice King

For years the skin hung loose on my bones and the teeth
which could have saved me rattled in their sockets.
My thick, white coat couldn't disguise the onset of
starvation. I hunted in vain, until early one morning
something strange and new appeared on the ice. I was
afraid, but desperation drove me on and then there were
screams and the certainty of death. I lashed out, terrified,
wishing that I had run away. My emaciated body was shot
through, of course, and hope for the Arctic died that day.

*On an expedition to Svalbard, in Norway, a sleeping
teenager was killed and four injured by a starving polar
bear who entered their tent in August 2011.*

Ignorance is bliss

'Nature is red in tooth and claw,' said my mother as we walked to school, myself shedding tears at the tragedy which had unfolded in the guinea pig shed during the night. Rats had gnawed into their wooden cage and left my bonny favourite dead and her gentle companion mortally wounded. Nevertheless, my darlings had put up a feisty fight and seen them off.

'It's not fair,' I wept.

'Life's not fair,' said my mother.

We walked on in miserable silence.

Thus I learned a fundamental truth, and now many years later I know that the same truth governs our entire lives.

In loving memory

I'll never forget that bullfight. We were protesting in
Vélez Málaga, Spain, in 2007 at their plans to turn
the temporary bullring into a permanent one. The
matadors—called *Toreros* over there—weren't even
famous and of course they ignored us, but you have to
be arrogant to parade for the crowd in all that glitz. They
dragged out about five or six bodies before I left and as
time went on the victims were noticeably smaller. In a
place like Vélez, no-one's too fussy about the rules and
the crowd likes value for money.

The young ones

There are things that happen outside the bullring which are equally terrible to what goes on inside. At least, relatively speaking. For instance, did you know that matadors practise their art by working their way along lines of calves? Like clumsy executioners of old, there are those who make many attempts at a kill before they succeed, effectively stabbing the forehead of the terrified calf again and again. So take pity on the persecuted bulls who are savaged in the ring for entertainment, but also spare a thought for the precursors to the sacred art of culture for the uncultured.

Karma

Since 1950 humans have produced 8.3 billion tonnes of plastic and the vast majority of it ends up as waste. Around 13 million metric tonnes of plastic rubbish is dumped into the ocean every year—about a truckload for every minute—and the devastation kills at least 100,000 marine mammals annually, including turtles, dolphins and whales. Death might take any number of forms but it is often the result of ingesting deadly plastic microbeads which enter the food chain at plankton level and work their way up. Given the destructive nature of the human species, it's hard to see why we deserve to survive.

Lawnmowers of the Savannah

Who would have thought that the comical hippo is one of the most dangerous animals in Africa? Or that they produce up to 27 kilos of liquid dung a day which they eject with varying momentum and no regard for whoever is in the firing line? But give or take the odd victim, most of it goes in the river where it acts as a fertiliser and produces superfood for insects and fish larvae which is then passed up the food chain and drives the river eco-system. As unsung heroes go, hippos are up there with the best of them.

Living dangerously

Bees are in danger of extinction and as far as important species go, there is probably no other single more important creature. If they disappeared we would lose all the crops and other plants that they pollinate, all the animals that eat those plants and so on to the top of the food chain—us. If they disappeared our supermarkets would be lucky to stock even half the amount of fruit and vegetables they have at present, but quite apart from all that, wouldn't it simply be a tragedy in itself to lose such a fascinating and industrious creature?

Living through genocide

A major factor in the decline of bees is the pesticides used in intensive farming. Even just down the road from my house in rural Cambridgeshire I was shocked in 2017 by the bizarre sight of thousands of dead bees lining the roadside at Barton. Behind the hedge was a field growing crops. People can help reverse this travesty by campaigning for a permanent ban on neonectonid pesticides, supporting local hives and by planting nectar rich flowers, of which there is a list on page 65.

Mad Eye

One eye was swollen and diseased, but the rest of you was beautiful and serene. It was probably a kick or a glancing blow from a car, because the other eye was green and perfect. You were young, not even a teenager yet, living with your family on the beach in La Cala. You didn't seem to be in pain and there were no protests when I put you in the car and took you to Rafa, who was busy as usual. He rang me later and offered to put you down or operate. I wish with all my heart I'd kept you and now my heart is where you live on.

Man's best friend

I gazed, dumbstruck, at the ancient truck which rattled slowly down the dirt track. My brain was numb, but my eyes saw hundreds of dogs spilling out of the open-top rear—some alive, some in-between, some dead for lack of air. A few tried to raise their heads a little, but there was no strength in their broken bodies and their staring eyes spoke only of man's inhumanity. At the end of the track lay a violent death and a single line on a restaurant menu.

In Vietnam and other parts of Asia dogs are reared for meat by villagers and also stolen by dog thieves.

Moral greatness

Gandhi said 'The greatness of a nation and its moral progress can be judged by the way its animals are treated.' This is never truer than of animals killed for their fur— whether trapped in the wild or reared in tiny, barren, wire cages for a product which nobody needs. The wearing of fur has been deemed unacceptable in Britain for some years but the fur trade is a ruthless, unprincipled bully with powerful friends and countries which are the main focus of current campaigns include the US, Canada and Iceland. The inspirational anti-fur organisation *Respect for Animals* has won many battles, but the war isn't over yet.

More than skin deep

I'm an African giant pouched rat, I weigh a whole kilo, I'm intelligent and I've got a sharper sense of smell than dogs. It's sad that so many people are judgemental and blinkered about us rats, because my kind are providing a service which makes our lives more worthy than those of any of our detractors. We've already cleared Mozambique of mines and are now doing the same for Cambodia, which still has as many as 5 million of them. We're not only a highly trained, elite force, but also irreplaceable.

Dogs doing the same work weigh more than five kilos, which is all it takes to set off a mine.

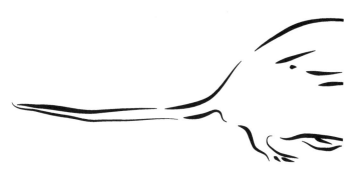

Mother love

The dairy farmer wiped his eyes, one arm half slung across the withers of a doe-eyed Jersey cow. 'I won't do it,' he muttered, half to himself.

'Won't do what?' enquired the government vet, staring across the countryside with unseeing eyes.

'They're healthy. Look at them!'

'We can't risk the infection spreading. You'll get compensation.'

'There *is* no bloody infection here. How can you stop what doesn't exist?'

His visitor turned away, disinterested, then jumped violently as a loud explosion rang out behind him. When he turned back the farmer was dead, his brains liberally spattered over the vet's crisp, designer anorak.

In response to the 1996 BSE crisis, when healthy herds were needlessly slaughtered in horrific conditions by hastily commandeered and untrained squaddies.

Naked truths

Humanity has wiped out 60% of animals globally since 1970.

The wildlife population in Britain is down 89% in the same time frame.

Freshwater wildlife populations in Britain have fallen by 83%.

Ninety per cent of 186 species of seabirds have plastic in their stomachs.

South and Central America are the worst affected by deforestation.

So says the *World Wildlife Fund 2018 Living Planet Report*, and yet despite the devastating figures, they cite windows of opportunity. Their stoicism requires reserves of energy and optimism that all of us would do well to emulate.

Next, please

Andrew Marr is probably my favourite journalist, but his 2018 Christmas Eve Radio 4 programme nevertheless marred my festive season, (pun intentional). One of his guests was the author Michelle Paver whose 2010 ghost story *Dark Matter* was set in the 1930s Arctic, and among the gems of her research was the Inuit solution to sled dogs chewing their harness. As a preventative measure they were routinely hung upside down until sufficiently woozy and then at least some of their molars knocked out with a hammer. I wonder if today's Arctic dentistry is any more refined.

On the bright side...

The world is on the brink of a collapse of civilisation caused by deep recession, according to a Cambridge academic based at the *Centre for the Study of Existential Risk* at the *University of Cambridge.* He analysed the lifespans of nearly 100 historic empires from Egypt to the Byzantine Empire and attributed their demise to climate change, environmental abuse and inequality. He backed up his theory with data showing the sinking American, Chinese and European economies. However, the average lifespan of civilizations studied was 336 years—by which standard we've done rather well, so let's not complain.

Turning the tide...

The Chinese market seller grinned vapidly for the camera as she clutched an endangered Pangolin tightly by the scruff of the neck, its four short paws spread-eagled and its mouth open in a scream of terror. Nearby on the dirt-encrusted market floor, two other females sat cross legged, working busily and every few seconds throwing another skinned rodent onto the huge pile of flesh accumulating next to them.

Billions of humans are culturally conditioned to feel little or no empathy for other creatures and Coronavirus is just one example of how nature will take her revenge.

Over to you

A surge in human populations, poaching and climate change are the main three causes of the decline in other species.

Steps need to be taken to reduce pollution and the negative impact of invasive species as these are the fourth and fifth biggest factors in the destruction of the natural world.

Financial incentives which damage biodiversity should be discredited and ignored.

There should be no more destructive subsidies for fossil fuels and industrial fishing and agriculture—these are what drive the plundering of the land and ocean.

At least a third of our land and sea needs to be protected, with 30% of that amount to be secured by 2030 and 50% by 2050.

IPBES report for governments

By the same author: to be published December 2020
101 words to save us from ourselves.

Around 60 soundbites about the enormous
environmental damage and animal cruelty involved
in intensive farming and the growing popularity of
veganism as one of the solutions.

Printed in Great Britain
by Amazon

59230916R00054